PARTIAL CLARITIES

PARTIAL CLARITIES

poetry

Tom McSorley

ELBORO

PARTIAL CLARITIES Copyright © 2021 by Tom McSorley

All rights reserved. No part of this book may be used or reproduced in any manner whatsoever without written permission except in the case of brief quotations embodied in critical articles and reviews.

ISBN: 978-1-7321817-3-1

Published in New York City by Elboro Press

Elboro Press books may be purchased in bulk for educational, business or sales promotional use. Please address enquiries to:

office@elboropress.com

Elboro Press
779 Riverside Drive, Suite B25
New York NY 10032

First Edition, 2021 – Second Printing

> It is only in isolate flecks that
> something
> is given off

William Carlos Williams, "*To Elsie*"

Contents

Room 183, Chateau Laurier	3
Room 2116 West	5
Will	7
Ten Years Today	9
Borges Alone	11
Winter Rabbit, Spruce Street	13
Carriage	15
Montréal vu par	17
Adolescence	19
Always	21
Auditor	23
Authorship	25
Correspondence	27
Goalie Haiku	29
End of Term	31
Guitar Lesson	33
Caretaker Motions	35
Learning Italian	37
An Approach to WD-40	39
Teacher	41
Movie Star	43
Late Morning October	45
Book Report	47
Anxiety of Influence	49
Togetherness	51
The Limited Gifts of Bacchus	53
Matching Pair	55
Happy Hour	57
Rosie and Her New Neighbor	59
Thought and Action	61
Chimney Sweeps	63
Mom's Birthday	65
Thinking Ahead	67
Silly Rhyming Overtime Loss	69
Life Lesson	71
Sad Fuck	73
On His Edges	75

River	77
Astronomy	81
Civilization, Pont du Gard	83
For LC at 80	85
How Long Do Horses Live?	87
The Word Made Flesh on a City Bus	89
Twelfth Critical Balcony, Film Festival	91

Partial Clarities

ROOM 183, CHATEAU LAURIER
(for my father)

When your eyes opened
You saw the ceiling of the room your body would
not let you leave.
Curtains moving near an open window.
The chair you like so far away.

When your mouth was open
you asked the room for more air, please.
Your tie and suspenders just so;
your cane bemused against the wall.

The food arrives and it is good.
You can manage this.
Your wife upset by your state;
you busy reassuring everyone with your tired smile.

ROOM 2116 WEST,
MIRAMICHI REGIONAL HOSPITAL

From her bed with tubes
going in and out of her,
in the small hard fear of her body's collapse
she looks out hospital windows at blue skies
observing in silence
that the weather has improved
that today is nicer than yesterday
that there is no wind
that the clouds are not moving.

WILL

From somewhere up on the source of
the river of time
will flow a gift
from before and after her,

a gift arriving unexpected
carried on quietly to gently swirl around me
from my feet to my heart to my sorrowful mind

easing slightly this
ache of yearning and memory
softened smile at the sound
of her name: Veronica

TEN YEARS TODAY

Uncertain
hard arrival
new pathways

unfamiliar staircase
cramped provisional
apartment

apart ago
ahead soon
maybe what

table and keys
standing there still
wondering

BORGES ALONE

When you perceive
that no one is watching
you reach calmly
for the tiny cup.

Tipping its warm surface
to your strange lips
you taste a marvelous
and hot liquid.

Is it in this
extravagant moment that you
forget your infinite
architecture of thought?

WINTER RABBIT, SPRUCE STREET

Brown silhouette on darkening snow
keeps alert distance
crunching sound approaching

stillness
obscure intentions
a quickening
now gone

CARRIAGE

the train rocks gently
white winter siding
drawn along by dark charcoal lines
beneath its cold wheels
steaming in hard sunshine
delivering actions and thoughts
moving warm limbs
cold stares sleepy distractions
shuddering across an alabaster terrain
its cargo of yearning

MONTRÉAL VU PAR

this city has moved on
always in motion
orbiting around its mountain
heading ever down that river

stop stopping
start starting

you were here then
as were they
you are here again
they are elsewhere

this simple spatial temporal
principle is the elastic undercarriage
of cities, of others, of you

ADOLESCENCE

I wonder how she does it,
hoping it is being done
to help clarify at least one
confusion she can manage,
my daughter who text messages me
less meaningfully less often.

ALWAYS

Preparing to speak to write to play to love to help to reassure to judge to censure to approve to read to look to look away to leave to arrive to stay to lose to triumph almost to sing to listen to weep to remember to laugh to project to prepare.

AUDITOR

this music mirror
bending time
signatures dopplering
away from toward
your one two three four
now and then and next

its sound is its own
apart abstract

yet its major minor
vibrates those small tender
drums of the skull
measuring somehow a
shimmering acoustic
outline of you

AUTHORSHIP

Arriving alongside a nearby conversation
I see a naked man in the change room with pocked
sagging buttocks talking about power.
It corrupts, he says knowingly
to his semi-clad heavy-set interlocutor.
Same old story, naked man continues, just like the
    Russian Revolution.
Then he asks, have you read, *Animal Farm*?

Semi-clad has not heard of it.
Naked carries on, the book by Orson Welles,
Orson Welles?... He ponders.
No, that English guy, right? Yes, H.G. Wells.
Semi-clad still has not a glimmer, but listens.

I consider a literary intervention
in the name of naming; but why? Naked man
understands the allegory and conveys it to semi-clad
who, now fully dressed, edges towards the exit.
My clothes are pulled on quickly, too, to avoid
any possible elaboration of this exchange.
I walk out into gentle February evening snows
thinking, no harm done and maybe even some good.

Orwell wasn't his real name anyway.

CORRESPONDENCE

your letter spoke
a fear of losing touch after our elders die off
you wrote your words
on torn scribbler paper
white with blue lines faint margins

they are gone, no one to send letters
to tell nothing of everything weather
us—if we are us anymore
—your scrawl says simply

fearing my and our vanishing
blank abandoned pages
clotted ink shaken to pages
hand awkwardly writes back
from a brink now illuminated

my marked stamp licked
warmed words enveloped
wait for collection
from the bottom
of an empty frosted
red metal mailbox
anticipating
your eyes someday

GOALIE HAIKU

he watches the game
sometimes the puck goes by him
thinking about life

END OF TERM

Would his last living
memory
be of this room,
a room in which
he stood speaking
over and over and over
some same some new things
as they came and went
year after year
awkward approach after awkward smile
sheepish shy solely aging
age accomplishment
while preparing to depart
this room
finally forever
leaving him to recall
remember
in a hush of empty desks
the chalk dust settling
under faltering fluorescent lights

again now
about to speak

GUITAR LESSON

the shapes of sound
under small fingers
upon hard metal strings
strummed in
your discovery
smiling

a code
to be cracked
a door into new rooms
as you grow slowly
up into your house
of life

CARETAKER MOTIONS

I love how you care
for this world enough
to stop stoop and pick up litter
with a frown at those who do
such thoughtless things
as your chocolate sinewy
hair sweeps across your
face as you rise into
your smile

LEARNING ITALIAN

These many new words
in your mouth are
chewed with difficulty
but slowly begin to taste
more familiar
digestible
with the scent
of flavour in those
new muscles discovered
in your throat, lips
and smiling cheeks
struggling to straddle
vowels and consonants

AN APPROACH TO WD-40

aching metal bike
croaks along the river
asking why am I so slow
to lubricate
accelerate change
rather than plow
through this known
noisy not-so-perfect
now

TEACHER
(for Peter Harcourt)

He stood there talking
And we began to hear our voices respond

He sat there writing
And our own hands were nudged in that direction

In the dark cinema he would laugh
We wondered if we could do this, or if we should

Beyond the solid skein of black marks on white paper
We wanted to avoid his puzzling personal storms

When the body was a swollen rubble fallen
We searched for traces of us somewhere in the pile

And soon laid out all words stilled at the end of his breathing
We struggled now to honour his deep silence with our sounds

MOVIE STAR

A main character
strides through the
scene

past a topless dancer
on her makeshift table

past a glass of apple juice
pretending to be beer

past an extra in the background
with his dim cinematic destiny

grazed by a camera
after brighter things

he, a gray array of blur

LATE MORNING OCTOBER
(for my mother)

Some gray October late morning
this music playing
shaping the warm amber light
around my fingers chattering on the keyboard
and outside cold rains sowing
seeds of snows imminent

I yearn for you to be there
putting things in order
in your far away small kitchen
while your husband is out
for a smoke and coffee at the
local diner down the road
you with your afternoon all ahead of you
a nap and line dancing with friends
whose limbs like yours are
stiffening up but still nimble
dark river water ever moving
outside those dance studio windows
as the town's cracked streets brace
for the coming of winter

Back here and now my day persists
this fine music that summoned
your image will soon resolve itself into silence
that now cloaks your distant stone grave
by the mute mirror witness of a river that
you loved, lived and died beside.

BOOK REPORT

Who knew one book
could contain so many stories?
As we wrestle to simplify a retelling
we marvel at how a Hardy Boys book
holds so much together in its small binding—
how imagination itself defies a summary,
reveals to us how we are taught
to build containers for our ideas
and call them thought.

That is what frustrates my son (and me)
as he struggles to finish his report:
knowing what it is he is leaving out.

ANXIETY OF INFLUENCE
(for Maya)

In the thickets of expressions
of others
I search to
perceive
my
own

and
me

TOGETHERNESS
(for Tina)

You witness a heaving
shuddering sadness in
our lovely kitchen,
shoulders that you love
curving and shaking
into suddenly trembling torso

Wondering: how did his shoulders carry
such vague insubstantial heavy rubble?
where was all this buried?
were you somehow brandishing
a shovel that disinterred
all these confused longings?
have you sown them
with your faulty expressions
of love and fear?

Soon: he tells you no—
it is his life's splintering
he is attempting to repair,
unsure as you are
(for different reasons)
as to why his talents
are so limited
his reparations so
well-intentioned yet
so partial.

THE LIMITED GIFTS OF BACCHUS

A winter night at year's end
I sip a smiling light white wine
—imported from Greece to
our infernal cold climate—
whispering firmly to my
troubled absent friend that he
has to stop drinking

                but

wanting to get drunk and tell him I love him
wishing he could muster a similar phrase and
shove it in my direction across
some old weathered bar
that has felt the spillages of human silence
stain the moments when such sentiments
could be easily safely spoken.

MATCHING PAIR

These threadbare socks
have no sentimental
value
except that now
you are carefully folding
them as you shake
your head

HAPPY HOUR

She liked how he said "interstitial,"
how it came from his mouth
suggested he might know
about many things that
lie in between other things—
that he's thought about them.

Tipping the glass tumbler
a cascade of ice to her lips
as sweet bitter final Negroni filmy
slithered from slackened cubes—
a slight involuntary eyebrow rises
silent expectant seduction concealed barely.

ROSIE AND HER NEW NEIGHBOR

Two cats stare
at one another
through glass
estranged—
wondering, I suppose,
how the other one
got there,
and what
to do
about it.

THOUGHT AND ACTION
(for William D. MacGillivray on the occasion of his 70th birthday)

He wasn't thinking of this.

Words came; images too; as they do.
But they weren't what he was thinking about:
Not his own aging, not of losses of those he
    loved—
because he knew,
with equanimity and acceptance,
that they would die;
they did naturally so.

Sadness. That wasn't it, either.

He was wrapped around in and by others who
loved him nourished him cherished him,
as he did them. He whistled his luck across
windy dawns, bright or cloudy mornings.
He counted those damned blessings.
No, that's not what he was thinking about.

It was more the uncanny accumulation
of surprise of opportunity of disappointment of
    failure of success
of strange loyalties arrayed around him—
that is what he began to think about.
He had no idea, nor needed to have, where his
    words and
images splintered off to and arrived at
    ultimately,
or whether they changed anyone for the better
    or worse,

or even a vague sense that at least they were not useless.
All he had done, kept on doing, was open his windows
breathe some kind of air, obscurely inspiring himself,
activating a yearning in others who want to breathe, too—
that air they describe as they pass through it,
the very fact that they are there
open hungry articulate.

But he wasn't thinking of this. He didn't need to.

What he had done was already beyond his thoughts,
beyond his long burned off need
to think about his thoughts;
those ashes of his faraway fire
that leave a pleasant incomplete residue.

Others, though (including me), were thinking of this, of him.
He had reached for a northern window latch, for he knew no other,
corroded by lashing salted gnarling Atlantic murmuring,
fearlessly opened it wide—
oceans now so permitted came rushing in
beautiful ferocious tender unformed;
without knowing how
—or even meaning to—
he has taught us
and himself
how to swim.

CHIMNEY SWEEPS

Rock chimneys out there
under the St. Lawrence River
scrape the hulls of ships passing above
gritty whispering
warning nautical designs
of primeval disorder
pulsing upward from
that core cauldron—
scratching admonishments
to maritime ambition.

MOM'S BIRTHDAY

Ninety-five seems like forever
and it is; and it is not.
She arrived before many things:
long distance telephone calls,
the Great Depression, World War II,
Hiroshima, Medicare, television,
Pierre Elliott Trudeau,
the internet.

She witnessed her eternity; she adjusted to it
time after time; she led or followed
her life for the first time, as we
all must do; it was so very
long, but it ended like a final
swallow of Canadian Club and water:
inevitable, surprising, too soon.

She almost made it to ninety;
she'd by ninety-five (a fine sounding number)
today.

Her death is now as eternal as her
life. I miss her company, yesterday
today tomorrow forever.

THINKING AHEAD

Many years on,
brand names
once so compelling
fall quietly to dust,
that scent on your wrist
so seductive now inert
residue of hope or lust
or thoughts that your
powers of persuasion and attraction
would preserve you intact through
all that heated human battle,
all that searching for some integration
you seemed to be promised
by a world you recognized as yours—
only now you and the world
are estranged across
teeming distractions
blurred cartographies
time's cruel lingering fade.

SILLY RHYMING OVERTIME LOSS

Down on one knee
down on his luck
a loss in overtime
a punch he couldn't duck;

coach says he's proud
cleats signed with dirt,
his crestfallen team embraces,
wrestling lessons from this hurt;

there is emotion in dull October air
a trembling in adult voices
the player shakes in sadness
at his sport's cruel choices.

LIFE LESSON

No nonsense: this life is to be led.

His father hesitates to speak on
    love
when the dust of
    poverty
threatens to settle;
to accumulate crushing
sedimentary pressure
that will flatten all things
comforting or tender.

Such a lesson must not
be withheld; these
emotional distances will
protect, not harm—
all wounds are healed
in slowly binding
hardness.

SAD FUCK

In a bare bulb sadness
where you think
you deserve
to be.

ON HIS EDGES
(for Ben)

From one angle
see shadowy upper lip
softly smudged by voice
deepening;

still, he curls on couch
under blanket,
staring into that
phone screen's
relentless distraction;

flickering comfort
against an adult world
coming hard for him,
and soon.

RIVER
(in memory of Françoise-Nicole Tremblay)

Morpheus whispers along the
widening Saint Lawrence
"It is time to go," while
this ancient water's grand unstoppable
caress of the shoreline
wears it away.

I recall the elegance
with which you
fixed your hair
in that Montréal kitchen mirror,
the way you admired the
aging shape of your flesh
under stylish brown clothes
which—as you knew—cloaked
those shifts and imperfections
time inscribes on the body.
Cigarette and wine balanced
in one hand
you stood before me
absorbed in your woman's business,
a free hand adjusting
your already perfect head.

I recall the shimmer
of your face
above a plush line of fur
on your winter coat
with the crunch of snow beneath our feet
as your small dog wiggled through
winter's passageways;

and the heat came in the
kitchen afterwards,
and smells of butter and wine,
lotions that soothed
dried skins, the
table's soft illumination,
and our diving like dolphins
in and out of *les langues
de Moliere et Shakespeare,*
the compassionate concentration
of your smile; the quiet, sweet concern
that things go well, that the food is good.

And I wondered about you
downriver now making life
*pour la suite du monde
l'Outaouais et Saint-Laurent*—
always flowing, always fleeing
out to the Atlantic,
always remaining,
insisting with their dark
essential *tableaux vivants*
under the snows, the dirty ice,
the rain, the obscure evaporations—
Ottawa flows into Montréal
into Québec City into Rimouski
and just around the Gaspé corner
a path to the ocean and
le vieux pays.

Today on this wintry spring day in March
I am unable to recall the last
time I saw you.
I tell myself it does not matter,

for with the beloved
first and last meetings are as one.

Then I imagine a memory—
a memory of some veil of haunted
stricken flesh melting over your
adamantine spirit and beauty,
Morpheus calling softly and
your river waiting for when
the annual ice it bears
will shudder and collide,
wander and dissolve,
making space in its universe of time
for your soft, ashen
return.

ASTRONOMY

My brother showed me
Jupiter
from the rooftop of
my reconstructed
heart
which he had helped
to heal without trying,
simply by placing
my eye upon the viewfinder
and calmly
telling me where
to look in
the night sky.

CIVILIZATION, PONT DU GARD

the Romans knew
that to shape
    a world
you must make heavy
stones arch their
backs into ancient air
and coax water
to go where you
want it to,
    because
you have plans for it

FOR LC AT 80

So much acclaim now
    An old singer cannot stop
Melodies of hope

HOW LONG DO HORSES LIVE?

Old horse
dies tall
in wood
whirling stall

down equine
universes of
effort motion
mute loyalty
muscular carriage

detonating
heart

THE WORD MADE FLESH ON A CITY BUS

Young woman
multiple pale scars
on hairy forearms
extend back from strong
hands holding
a worn paperback
open pages caressed
word by word
by a thumb
guiding rapt eyes
away from days
when her arms
spoke blood
beneath a
razor's tongue.

TWELFTH CRITICAL BALCONY, FILM FESTIVAL
(for G.P.)

mist heavy
fog is down
clings to
savage ironic
talk

city lights
trace earthly
constellations and
follow thoughts
out into night

a fashion cigarette
dips from your sad lips,
clouds your arbiter's eyes
as we speak
about
this rigid irredeemable
world

softened now by
distant
autumnal fog
pale light
and
fine impotent
language

www.ingramcontent.com/pod-product-compliance
Lightning Source LLC
Chambersburg PA
CBHW071020080526
44587CB00015B/2437